Looking At Women Is Not A Sin

Proven From The Bible

Rich Newman

Scripture quotations marked CJB are from the Complete Jewish Bible. Copyright © 1998 by David H. Stern. Published by Jewish New Testament Publications, Inc. Used by permission.

Scripture quotations marked GWN are from GOD'S WORD® translation. Copyright © 1995 by God's Word to the Nations. Used by permission.

Scripture quotations marked KJV are from the King James Version of the Bible.

Scripture quotations marked LXE are from The English Translation of The Septuagint Version of the Old Testament by Sir Lancelot C. L. Brenton, 1844, 1851. Published by Samuel Bagster and Sons, London.

Scripture quotations marked NET are from The NET Bible, Version 1.0. Copyright © 2004, 2005 Biblical Studies Foundation. Used by permission.

Scripture quotations marked NIV are from THE HOLY BIBLE: NEW INTERNATIONAL VERSION®. Copyright © 1973, 1978, 1984 by International Bible Society. Used by permission of Zondervan Publishing House.

Scripture quotations marked NLT are from the Holy Bible, New Living Translation. Copyright © 1996. Used by permission of Tyndale House Publishers.

Copyright © 2009 by Rich Newman. All rights reserved.

CFA Publications
Box 702032, Tulsa, OK 74170 USA
www.CFApublications.com

Library of Congress Control Number: 2009922346
Library of Congress subject headings:
Sexual ethics — Biblical teaching.
Adultery — Biblical teaching.
Sin — Biblical teaching.
Lust — Religious aspects — Christianity.
Sex — Biblical teaching.
Sex — Religious aspects — Christianity — Biblical teaching.
Christian men — Sexual behavior.
Sex in the Bible.

ISBN 978-0-9822097-0-7

I dedicate this book to Jesus Christ, Who, because He loved us more than He loved Himself, came to earth to set us all free, not to put us into bondage.

Thanks

I deeply appreciate everyone who helped me with this book. And those who have supported me and encouraged me through the years. Thank you! May God richly bless you all!

Contents

Preface 9
Introduction 11
1 The Translation Problem 17
2 The Bible Meaning Of Adultery 23
3 "Woman" Should Be Translated "Wife" 31
4 Lust Is Not A Sin 35
5 "Lust After" Should Be Translated "Covet" 51
6 What Is Sin? 55
7 Conclusion: Looking At Women Is Not A Sin 79
Even If You Have Sinned, You Can Be Forgiven 85
Why I Am Selling This Book 91
Afterword 97
Bibliography 99

Preface

MATTHEW 5:28 KJV
28 But I say unto you, That whosoever looketh on a woman to lust after her hath committed adultery with her already in his heart.

- Do you wish this verse was not in the Bible?

- Have you ever felt guilty when you looked at a beautiful woman, because you thought Jesus said you were not supposed to look at women?

- Do you feel condemned for the feelings you have whenever you see a beautiful woman?

- Does it seem impossible for you to resist looking at women, no matter how hard you try?

- Do you feel like a poor excuse for a Christian because of the thoughts and desires you have every time you see a beautiful woman?

- Have you felt like you could never get victory over lust?

- Have you been plagued with guilt and shame because you have been unable to overcome your desire to look at women?

- Are you tired of confessing the same old sin to the Lord, knowing you have no power or ability to stop doing it?

If you answered yes to any of these questions, please read this book to find out the truth of what Jesus said, and what Jesus meant. Victory and freedom can be yours!

> JOHN 8:32 KJV
> 32 And ye shall know the truth, and the truth shall make you free.

Introduction

First, let me introduce myself. I am a Bible-believing, Christian follower of Jesus Christ. I am not a sex pervert. And I am not looking to find some loophole in Scripture so I can spend my days looking at pictures of naked women. My primary focus and motivation in life is to know God and do His will. I accept the teaching of God's Word, the Bible, as the final authority in my life.

Pleasing God is my desire. I don't believe we should live our lives on the outer edge of God's will, trying to get away with as much as we can without receiving His rebuke. Instead, I believe God is good and His way is best for us, so we should desire and endeavor to live in the center of God's will.

I am a lifelong student, always interested in learning. My quest however, is a desire to know truth, not just human tradition.

The ideas in this book were initially quite a shock to me. My church background did not prepare me to readily accept these ideas. In fact they seemed dangerous to me. So I struggled whether to share the teaching in this book, out of concern it might somehow hinder someone in their walk with Christ.

My thinking — like nearly every Christian man today — was colored by church tradition and Bible language that caused me to be on guard against, and highly suspect of anything sexual. Our tradition seems to label everything having to do with sex — even a thought — as sin. The thinking seems to be that sex is somehow dirty — certainly the opposite of godly or holy — although I didn't really understand why. This just seems to be part of our Christian culture in the twenty-first century.

Our world is saturated with sexuality. But most people think Jesus is against sex. Christianity is certainly viewed as a sex-negative religion. But this is not the true message of the Bible. And certainly not the message communicated by our great Creator through the glorious creation we see all around us (Romans 1:20).

So I finally concluded the teaching in this book is needed because there are so many in the Body of Christ who struggle in their relationship with God because they feel condemned over their sexual thoughts and feelings. Because of a misunderstanding of God's requirements, they think they can never measure up to God's standards. So they are crippled in their spiritual growth, feeling they can never have God's approval, creating a huge barrier to the relationship God desires to have with each one of them.

This book is to help men know the truth, so they will no longer be kept from enjoying close fellowship with Jesus Christ – who loves every man more than they can possibly imagine.

Let's get started by looking at Matthew 5:28.

> MATTHEW 5:28 KJV
> 28 But I say unto you, That whosoever looketh

on a woman to lust after her hath committed adultery with her already in his heart.

When you read Matthew 5:28 in any modern English Bible, it seems as clear as the nose on your face that Jesus taught that just looking at a woman and being attracted to her is a sin.

But Jesus did not say that. Neither did Jesus mean that. And this book will prove it from Scripture, beyond any doubt.

The problem has been not understanding the meaning of the Greek words used to translate the words woman, lust, and adultery in our English Bibles.

The first thing we need to understand is that the word translated "woman" should be translated "wife." In fact, it is impossible in the context of who Jesus was speaking to, to correctly translate the word as woman, instead of wife. Chapter three will explain this.

To understand why it would be impossible to translate this correctly as woman instead of wife, we must study the subject of adultery as it was understood by the people Jesus was speaking to. This is covered in detail in chapter two.

Today, in our culture, adultery has the meaning of any sexual activity by a married person outside their marriage. But, although this may be a good definition, it is not what the people who heard Jesus speak these words originally would have understood by His use of the word "adultery."

Jesus was not introducing a new definition of adultery, or changing the Old Testament Law. He was only telling us that the sin actually started at the point when a person made the decision and started planning to commit the act. Motives and intent to do something make you guilty — not just if you commit the act and are caught. In God's sight you are guilty as soon as you decide to commit the sin.

In this verse we are dealing with one of the foundation blocks of western culture — which was wrongly understood. This misunderstanding is part of the reason why we tend to be embarrassed about sex and to consider it dirty and unspiritual, even though God created us as sexual beings and meant for us to enjoy all that He created.

Certainly, we must keep sexual activity within the proper bounds if we are to enjoy it as God designed and intended. But, doing so does not require us to place restrictions on ourselves that the Bible never places on us.

In this book all references are to males looking at women. But surely it is no different for a woman to look at a man, than for a man to look at a woman. It is not a sin for either men or women.

Although some women may be so insecure that they cannot stand for their man to look at any other woman, God doesn't have a problem with you looking and enjoying the view. Of course, if your woman is insecure and offended when you look at other women, then you should not do it, because that would not be obeying the command of Christ to love others, and especially to love your wife.

But, nowhere in the Bible does it teach that looking at women is a sin. So, read this book, and study it with your Bible open. Then share it with others, so we can all begin to enjoy all the beauty that God created, without guilt or shame.

Before you begin reading this book, I suggest you ask the Lord Jesus to open your understanding and show you the truth on this subject.

Chapter 1

The Translation Problem

The Bible is the inspired Word of God on which we can base our lives, and our eternal destiny, without fear. I am certain it is true and dependable, just like its Divine Author. It works for me in the practical matters of everyday life. Without any doubt I know that if you will believe the Bible, and act on it, your life will change for the better.

There is a small problem, but it is not insurmountable. All English Bibles are translations, not the original documents, and since all translators are human, sometimes their English translation is not perfect.

So, on some passages, to get the full and clear meaning, we have to dig deeper and study the words in the original languages. Fortunately, there are many English language tools to help us do that without having to be experts on those languages.

For the majority of Bible passages, this is not necessary. But some passages, like Matthew 5:28, require us to really do some very detailed study to find out the true meaning of what Jesus originally said.

> MATTHEW 5:28 KJV
> 28 But I say unto you, That whosoever looketh

on a woman to lust after her hath committed adultery with her already in his heart.

Did Jesus mean what He said?

Yes! But what did He mean?

The problem is that Jesus did not speak in English, so we have the obstacle of going from one language to another, which is further complicated by differences in our cultures and around two thousand years of time.

Originally, the books of the Bible were written in Hebrew or Greek. And words often change meaning over time. For example, just a generation ago, "gay" had a totally different meaning in English than it has today. You can imagine how much word usage could change in a period a hundred times longer.

For us to understand what God is saying to us in the Bible, we must study the words as they were used in the original language and context and find out what their meaning was to the people they were originally spoken to. This is not always an easy task. Sometimes it is almost impossible without divine help.

But Jesus promised the Holy Spirit would guide us into all truth, (John 16:13), so we can approach Bible study in faith as long as we trust in Him to guide us. Understanding the truth of the Bible requires more than Bible college degrees. The help of the Holy Spirit is absolutely necessary.

But you may say, "Isn't there some Bible translation I can trust? Surely, out of all the English versions, there must be one that got it right."

The Translation Problem

Unfortunately, while there are many fine English Bible translations, none are perfect. Nor is it likely there will ever be one that is perfect, unless Jesus does it Himself after His return to earth.

Translation is not an exact science. There are shades of meaning and subtle differences that are easily missed by someone who is not a native speaker of a language and who lived in that culture and time. Accurate translation, especially of the Bible, where every word is so vital, is exceedingly difficult.

Sometimes a translator is forced to paraphrase the original in order to get the full thought expressed accurately into English. All translators consciously or unconsciously make interpretations in their translations, no matter how hard they may try not to do so. After all, we are all human, and none of us knows everything.

Clarence Jordan in his Introduction to *The Cotton Patch Version of Paul's Epistles*[3] provides a thought-provoking example of the difficulty of understanding and translating something from another time and culture.

> "For example, someone would be perfectly understood if he wrote to a friend, 'We had hot dogs and Coke for lunch, fish and hush puppies for supper, and then sat around shooting the bull until midnight.' But let that letter get lost for about two thousand years, then let some Ph.D. try to translate it into a non-English language of A.D. 3967. If he faithfully translated the words it might run something like this: 'We had steaming canines (possibly a small variety such as the Chihuahua — Ed.) and processed coal (the coke was probably not

eaten but used to heat the dogs — Ed.) for the noon meal, and fish and mute, immature dogs (no doubt the defective offspring of the hot dog, with which twentieth-century Americans were so preoccupied — Ed.) for the evening meal, followed by passively engaging until midnight in the brutish sport of bull-shooting (the bulls were then processed into a large sausage called bologna, which sounded like "baloney" — Ed.).' For such scholarship the good doctor may have won world renown as the foremost authority on twentieth-century English — without having the slightest idea what was actually said!"

While all English Bibles are only translations done by fallible men, they are all valuable. Anyone who knows enough about Hebrew or Greek to translate the Scriptures, knows more than I do of those languages. So any intelligent person will realize they can learn something from all of them.

I appreciate every translation we do have, and the efforts of the translators who tried their best to bring us the Word of God in a language we can understand. Thank God for them!

None of this means we cannot trust the Bible. It just means that we sometimes have to put forth some extra effort to study and understand what God's accurate message to us is.

Continue In God's Word

Should you let this discourage you from reading and study of the Bible? No! Jesus promised that continuing in His Word would cause us to know the truth which would make us free. But we must continue. It is not enough to just read the Bible once and expect to have mastered and understood it completely.

> JOHN 8:31-32 KJV
> 31 Then said Jesus to those Jews which believed on him, If ye continue in my word, then are ye my disciples indeed;
> 32 And ye shall know the truth, and the truth shall make you free.

God's Word is alive and pays rich dividends as we study it.

> HEBREWS 4:12 NLT
> 12 For the word of God is alive and powerful. It is sharper than the sharpest two-edged sword, cutting between soul and spirit, between joint and marrow. It exposes our innermost thoughts and desires.

> 2 TIMOTHY 2:15 KJV
> 15 Study to shew thyself approved unto God, a workman that needeth not to be ashamed, rightly dividing the word of truth.

God does desire for us to understand His message, but He has purposely hidden away treasured insights for those who will seek Him and study His Word diligently.

> PROVERBS 2:3-5 KJV
> 3 Yea, if thou criest after knowledge, and liftest up thy voice for understanding;
> 4 If thou seekest her as silver, and searchest for her as for hid treasures;
> 5 Then shalt thou understand the fear of the LORD, and find the knowledge of God.

LUKE 24:45 KJV
45 Then opened he their understanding, that they might understand the Scriptures,

So, as you read and study the Bible, always do it prayerfully, asking the Lord to teach you and give you understanding. And remember to be humble, realizing that what you think — or what all Christians have thought for years — may be wrong. As the apostle Paul, who was caught up to Heaven, received direct revelation, and wrote down most of the New Testament, said in 1 Corinthians 13:9 "For we know in part."

My suggestion is that you use modern translations like devotional commentaries. Read them and let the Lord speak to you through them. But for detailed study in English, I suggest using the King James Version or the New King James Version (and the tools that are available to study the words used in them).

The important thing is not which Bible translation you use for reading, it is whether you act on the Bible truth you know and manifest the love of God to the world.

Chapter 2

The Bible Meaning Of Adultery

The seventh of the Ten Commandments seems clear and plain: do not commit adultery. Adultery is a sin, and God commanded people not to do it.

EXODUS 20:14 KJV
14 Thou shalt not commit adultery.

But the question is, what does the Bible mean by adultery? As we know, the meaning of words can change over time.

We know what society today considers adultery: any person having sexual intercourse outside their marriage. But our desire is to answer the question, "What does God and the Bible consider adultery?" (Especially in the Old Testament, as the New Testament was not yet written in the days when Jesus Christ ministered on earth, so the Old Testament was their "Bible," the standard of the people He spoke to.)

Study of the Bible does reveal adultery had a different meaning in Bible days. So, what is adultery according to the Bible?

Adultery according to the Old Testament always involved sex with a married woman who was the wife of another man. Whether a man was married, or not, was irrelevant. This is what adultery meant to the people to whom Jesus Christ spoke.

> LEVITICUS 20:10 KJV
> 10 And the man that committeth adultery with another man's wife, even he that committeth adultery with his neighbour's wife, the adulterer and the adulteress shall surely be put to death.
>
> DEUTERONOMY 22:22 KJV
> 22 If a man be found lying with a woman married to an husband, then they shall both of them die, both the man that lay with the woman, and the woman: so shalt thou put away evil from Israel.

According to the usage of the word adultery in the Old Testament, a man could only commit adultery with someone who is the wife of another man. If a married man had a sexual relationship with an unmarried woman, it was not considered adultery. For a man to commit adultery he had to have sex with a married woman who was not his wife. His marital status made no difference.

According to the Old Testament, for a woman to commit adultery, she had to be a wife (or betrothed as a wife, which they considered already being a wife), and she had to have sex with a man other than her husband.

Never does the Old Testament use the term adultery when a man had sex with a woman unless she was married to another man. (Yes, there was clearly a double standard allowing men to have sex with fewer restrictions than women were allowed. I am just stating what the Bible actually says on the subject.)

Sex With A Single Woman Not Adultery

The penalty for adultery was death for both the man and woman. But there was no penalty if a man — married or unmarried — had sex with an unmarried woman. He was, however, required to marry her, unless her father objected.

> EXODUS 22:16-17 KJV
> 16 And if a man entice a maid that is not betrothed, and lie with her, he shall surely endow her to be his wife.
> 17 If her father utterly refuse to give her unto him, he shall pay money according to the dowry of virgins.

Notice that this passage says nothing about the marital status of the man involved. Polygamy was widely practiced in the Bible, so, whether a man already had a wife, or not, made no difference in this situation. So, for a married man to have sex with a single woman, was not considered adultery. There was no death penalty, but rather the man had to marry the woman. (It may seem that there was a financial penalty of paying the "bride price" or "dowry" but that was the normal custom for all men to pay to the family of the woman they married. That was a normal part of marriage in their culture.)

Other Situations

> DEUTERONOMY 22:23-27 KJV
> 23 If a damsel that is a virgin be betrothed unto an husband, and a man find her in the city, and lie with her;
> 24 Then ye shall bring them both out unto the gate of that city, and ye shall stone them

with stones that they die; the damsel, because she cried not, being in the city; and the man, because he hath humbled his neighbour's wife: so thou shalt put away evil from among you.
25 But if a man find a betrothed damsel in the field, and the man force her, and lie with her: then the man only that lay with her shall die:
26 But unto the damsel thou shalt do nothing; there is in the damsel no sin worthy of death: for as when a man riseth against his neighbour, and slayeth him, even so is this matter:
27 For he found her in the field, and the betrothed damsel cried, and there was none to save her.

This passage shows us that a woman who was betrothed was already considered a wife, as far as adultery was concerned, even though she was still a virgin. If a man forced her to have sex while they were in the city, where others could hear her cries for help, and she did not cry out for help, they were both punished with death. If however, the act took place in the country, the woman was given the benefit of the doubt and only the man was put to death.

> DEUTERONOMY 22:28-29 KJV
> 28 If a man find a damsel that is a virgin, which is not betrothed, and lay hold on her, and lie with her, and they be found;
> 29 Then the man that lay with her shall give unto the damsel's father fifty shekels of silver, and she shall be his wife; because he hath humbled her, he may not put her away all his days.

The Bible Meaning Of Adultery

If a man — married or unmarried — forced sex with a single woman who was not betrothed, he was required to pay the woman's father the customary bride price or dowry. Furthermore, he was prohibited from ever divorcing her.

There is no punishment specified in the Old Testament for a man — married or not — having sex with a slave, a prostitute, a concubine, a widow, or a divorced woman, as long as she was not married to someone else. Please understand that I am not saying the Bible encouraged such behavior, but only that it was not considered adultery.

Sex With A Slave Wife Not Adultery

Another exception to the death penalty is having sex with a slave woman who is a wife. If a man — any man, married or single — had sex with a slave woman, even though she was betrothed to a husband, and thus his wife in their eyes, it was not considered adultery. There was no death penalty as there was for adultery. The man only had to pay a fine to the owner of the slave woman for the damage he had caused to her value.

> LEVITICUS 19:20 NLT
> 20 "If a man has sex with a slave girl whose freedom has never been purchased but who is committed to become another man's wife, he must pay full compensation to her master. But since she is not a free woman, neither the man nor the woman will be put to death.
>
> LEVITICUS 19:20-22 KJV
> 20 And whosoever lieth carnally with a woman, that is a bondmaid, betrothed to an husband, and not at all redeemed, nor freedom given her;

she shall be scourged; they shall not be put to death, because she was not free.
21 And he shall bring his trespass offering unto the LORD, unto the door of the tabernacle of the congregation, even a ram for a trespass offering. 22 And the priest shall make an atonement for him with the ram of the trespass offering before the LORD for his sin which he hath done: and the sin which he hath done shall be forgiven him.

So the Bible considers it a sin for a man to have sex with a "married" slave, because a trespass offering was required and a fine had to be paid to the slave owner. But there was no death penalty, so it was not considered adultery.

Because it specifically mentions that they shall not be put to death, it is obvious this was to make it clear that this was an exception to the general law of adultery. In other words, the same act, that if committed with a free wife would get you death for adultery, was not adultery when done with a slave woman. There really is no explanation for this other than to conclude that the law against adultery, in the Old Testament, had more to do with protecting property rights than it had to do with limiting sexual activity.

Property Rights

Our modern idea is that God's primary motive in His laws concerning sex was to prohibit any sexual expression outside of marriage, but a detailed study of the Law shows it had more to do with property rights, and treating all people fairly. (Modern women may not think those women were treated fairly at all, but they need to bear in mind that it was a very different culture and what may seem unfair to us today, could actually be a merciful provision for the time.)

One thing that makes me think adultery in the Old Testament was more of a property issue than a sexual issue is the fact that the penalty for what we would consider "adultery" with a slave was much lighter than adultery with a free woman.

> EXODUS 20:17 KJV
> 17 Thou shalt not covet thy neighbour's house, thou shalt not covet thy neighbour's wife, nor his manservant, nor his maidservant, nor his ox, nor his ass, nor any thing that is thy neighbour's.

The tenth commandment, in Exodus 20:17, includes coveting your neighbor's wife in the same category as coveting any of his property. This shows further the mindset of the people of the time concerning a wife being property belonging to her husband.

L. William Countryman in his book, *Dirt Greed & Sex, Sexual Ethics in the New Testament and Their Implications For Today*[1] says of adultery on page 157 that it "referred purely and simply to a man's having intercourse with a married woman. The man's own marital status was irrelevant, for it was not a matter of violating his own vows or implicit commitments of sexual fidelity, as in a modern marriage, but rather of usurping some other man's property rights in his wife."

Countryman continues on page 159 to say, "The understanding of adultery, both in the Torah and in the New Testament era, thus proves to have been quite different from that current in the contemporary Western world.""Again, our own explanations of what is wrong in adultery usually focus on the betrayal of trust and of formal commitments between spouses, whereas the ancient understanding of adultery assumes rather that it is a violation of another's property. What for us is analogous to betrayal was for them a species of theft. The treatment of adultery in the New Testament documents is almost certain to be unintelligible if we do not keep these distinctions in mind."

Readers should not take anything said in this chapter as advocating or encouraging looseness in sexual activity by anyone. Today we live in a different culture, and I am not suggesting everything that was acceptable then is acceptable, or beneficial, behavior now.

Our purpose here is not to judge or debate what the meaning of adultery should be today. It is only to determine what the word adultery meant to the people to whom Jesus Christ spoke. Their thinking came from the Old Testament use of the word adultery, which we have studied in this chapter.

Our conclusion has to be that no one in Israel during the earthly ministry of Jesus would have thought anything was adultery unless it involved sex with a married woman and some man who was not her husband. Period.

Chapter 3

"Woman" Should Be Translated "Wife"

The word translated as "woman" in Matthew 5:28 is one of those instances where some study has to be done to grasp the correct meaning.

To understand why the correct translation is "wife" in Matthew 5:28, instead of "woman," will require us to consider the thinking of the people to whom Jesus spoke this verse.

Bear in mind that our language is different, and our culture is different. Those who heard Jesus speak Matthew 5:28 originally, believed adultery had to involve a married woman. Otherwise, it was not adultery. So they would never have thought of any possibility of there being "adultery" with a woman who was not already someone's wife.

The Greek language, which the New Testament was originally written in, did not have different words for woman and wife. So, every time the translators came across this Greek word, they had to make a decision if the word wife or woman should be used in that particular verse.

The meaning had to be taken from the context in which the word was used. Also, the idea of whether it should be translated as singular or plural had to be determined from the context, as there was just one Greek word for both. That is why the King James translators used all four of these words, wife, wives, woman, and women, to translate the one Greek word, gyne.

The Greek word gyne (or gune) is used 268 times in the New Testament. In the King James Version of the Bible it is translated as wife 103 times, woman 118 times, wives 15 times, and women 32 times.

Here are some example verses to show how this Greek word was translated. The words in bold in the following four verses are all translated from "gyne" in the Greek New Testament.

> ACTS 5:14 KJV
> 14 And believers were the more added to the Lord, multitudes both of men and **women**.)
>
> EPHESIANS 5:28 KJV
> 28 So ought men to love their **wives** as their own bodies. He that loveth his **wife** loveth himself.
>
> 1 CORINTHIANS 7:33 KJV
> 33 But he that is married careth for the things that are of the world, how he may please his **wife**.
>
> LUKE 10:38 KJV
> 38 Now it came to pass, as they went, that he entered into a certain village: and a certain **woman** named Martha received him into her house.

The first time the New Testament was ever translated into English from the Greek was by William Tyndale in 1525. His translation done in 1534 is available today and translates this Greek word gyne correctly as wife.

"Woman" Should Be Translated "Wife"

Unfortunately, I have not found any modern English translation which correctly translates this word gyne in Matthew 5:28 as wife.

To know how to translate the word gyne in Matthew 5:28 correctly, you must have a clear understanding of what adultery meant in the Bible. When you understand that, you realize it would be impossible to correctly translate this word in this context as anything other than "wife."

For a detailed study of The Bible Meaning of Adultery, please see that chapter beginning on page 23. To repeat our conclusion from that chapter, no one in Israel during the earthly ministry of Jesus would have thought anything was adultery unless it involved sex with a married woman and some man who was not her husband. Period.

In Greek the word gyne can mean either "woman" or "wife." The translator must therefore make a choice on the basis of his understanding of the context.

> MATTHEW 5:28 KJV
> 28 But I say unto you, That whosoever looketh on a woman to lust after her hath committed adultery with her already in his heart.

The people Jesus spoke this to would never think of the possibility of adultery unless a married woman was involved. This is why the word gyne in Matthew 5:28 must be translated as wife (instead of woman), as that is the only possible meaning those who heard Jesus could have attached to it.

Once you realize that the only possible correct translation in this verse is "wife," it is easy to see that only looking at any woman cannot be what Jesus is calling the sin of adultery.

This error in understanding what Jesus meant has been a huge stumbling block, which should have never existed, and has generated many wrong teachings.

Chapter 4

Lust Is Not A Sin

The church has misunderstood what the Bible really teaches about lust.

Today we think of lust as mainly sexual desire, but in the Bible days the word meant any kind of desire, either good or evil.

If the Bible is true, and I believe it is, then lust is not a sin. One reason is because James 1:15 tells us that it is only when lust has "conceived" that sin is brought forth. So, lust can cause us to sin, if it takes control of us and causes us to act, but lust by itself is not a sin.

> JAMES 1:14-15 KJV
> 14 But every man is tempted, when he is drawn away of his own lust, and enticed.
> 15 Then when lust hath conceived, it bringeth forth sin: and sin, when it is finished, bringeth forth death.

An insight we can gain from this verse is that all sin is brought forth by lust. Obviously, there are many sins which are not sexual in nature, such as theft and murder, so lust cannot be confined to matters of sex only.

Just from the evidence in James 1:15, it should be clear that lust is not sin, but that it can bring forth, or produce sin. According to this verse, lust has to "conceive" and bring forth an act before it becomes a sin.

A concise definition of the Greek word which is translated as "conceived," sullambano, which fits all the occurrences of the word in the New Testament, is to take control of someone to get them to do something.

"Sullambano" is used in several different situations in the New Testament. What they all have in common is that someone or something else is taking control to accomplish some action. It is the normal word used for a woman who conceives a baby. The baby is taking control of her body, in a sense. It is also used of helping someone by taking hold of something together with them. But it is most often used with the meaning of arresting someone and taking them as a prisoner. All occurrences of the word include the idea of action, never of just thoughts.

So, it is only when lust has taken control of us and caused us to act that a sin happens.

> JAMES 1:14 NLT
> 14 Temptation comes from our own desires, which entice us and drag us away.

We must be on guard regarding lust, because lust has the ability to entice us and drag us away — to get us to do something wrong. But it is only when lust gets us to actually DO something that it becomes a sin.

Jesus Was Tempted

Temptation is not a sin. Jesus went through temptation, yet He did not sin, which proves that temptation is not a sin.

Lust Is Not A Sin

HEBREWS 2:18 KJV
18 For in that he himself hath suffered being tempted, he is able to succour them that are tempted.

MATTHEW 4:1 KJV
1 Then was Jesus led up of the Spirit into the wilderness to be tempted of the devil.

HEBREWS 4:15 KJV
15 For we have not an high priest which cannot be touched with the feeling of our infirmities; but was in all points tempted like as we are, yet without sin.

According to Hebrews 4:15 Jesus was tempted in every way we are tempted. For this to be true, and it is, that would certainly have to include the desire to have sex with someone it was not lawful for Him to have sex with. If Jesus did not face that temptation, then He certainly was not tempted in all the ways we are. Wouldn't you agree?

If you analyze it, without sexual desire (lust) there is no real temptation. Have you ever been tempted to have sex with someone when you had no sexual desire for them? Of course not! It is the presence of sexual desire that makes it a temptation. Without strong sexual desire, there is really no temptation to commit any sexual sin.

So, Jesus had to have strong sexual desire, for Him to be tempted in all the ways that we are. Yet the Bible is clear that He did not sin. So, strong sexual desire, or lust, cannot be sin because Jesus had it, yet did not ever sin.

> HEBREWS 4:15 NIV
> 15 For we do not have a high priest who is unable to sympathize with our weaknesses, but we have one who has been tempted in every way, just as we are — yet was without sin.

Lust is only the temptation, not the sin. It is only when lust takes control of you, forcing you into action, that sin results.

Don't Lust After What Belongs To Others

We should not "strongly desire" or lust after something or someone that is forbidden to us — what is not legal for us to have.

It may seem like Jesus in Matthew 5:28 is telling us that lust is sin — the sin of adultery. (There is no question that adultery is sin.)

> MATTHEW 5:28 KJV
> 28 But I say unto you, That whosoever looketh on a woman to lust after her hath committed adultery with her already in his heart.

What Jesus said is true. When you look at a wife with the desire and intention to take her away from her husband, then you have already committed adultery in your heart.

But Jesus is not saying that a thought is sin. Rather He is saying that once you have made the decision and have the intention to commit the act, you have already made the decision and all you lack is the opportunity to commit the sin.

Today English is the "universal language" used worldwide for trade, aviation, and international relations.

When Jesus walked the earth the Greek language was the "universal language" of that day. And the popular version of Scripture was the Septuagint, a Greek translation of the Old Testament, just like the King James Version has been an accepted and popular version in our time, so we are familiar with the words that it uses.

Keep in mind that the word translated lust in the New Testament, and used by Jesus here in Matthew 5:28, is the same word used in the Septuagint Greek Old Testament in the tenth commandment to not covet. So, this gives us insight that covet and lust are often used interchangeably in Scripture. And it also should be clear that the people who heard Jesus say this would think of the tenth commandment because of the same word being used.

God's law given in the tenth commandment does not say, "Do not covet." God did not give such a law! What the commandment does say is:

> EXODUS 20:17 KJV
> 17 Thou shalt not covet thy neighbour's house, thou shalt not covet thy neighbour's wife, nor his manservant, nor his maidservant, nor his ox, nor his ass, nor any thing that is thy neighbour's.

There is a big difference between saying "Do not covet." and "Do not covet what belongs to your neighbor!"

If it is wrong for us to covet (or desire) anything our neighbor has, that would mean it would be wrong for us to have any desire whatsoever. In that case, if your neighbor had water to drink and you wanted water to drink, it would be a sin, which it is not. That is not what the commandment means by "Do not covet what belongs to your neighbor." It is only saying you should not desire to take the water that belongs to your neighbor. There is nothing wrong with desiring to have your own water and digging a well to get your own water. That is a legitimate desire. It is only wrong when your desire is to take what belongs to your neighbor, and deprive him of it.

To illustrate, imagine you were a farmer in Israel. If your neighbor had sheep and cattle, would it be a sin for you to desire to have some sheep and cattle? If your neighbor had a wife and children, would it be a sin for you to desire to have a wife and children — even if it was a very strong desire?

No! All God commanded was not to desire to have your neighbor's wife, children, or property, with the intent to take them away from him.

Jesus even gave us directions in Mark 11:24 how we are to pray for what we desire. Asking God to give you what you desire is fine. Just don't ask God to give you what belongs to your neighbor!

> MARK 11:24 KJV
> 24 Therefore I say unto you, What things soever ye desire, when ye pray, believe that ye receive them, and ye shall have them.

In the New Testament, (in Romans 7:7 and 13:9) this commandment is written in the shortened form of "Do not covet," but you can be certain no devout Jewish person would intentionally dare to "take away from God's Word." Obviously, the commandment was written in the New Testament in a short form, assuming people knew the whole meaning.

Lust Is Used In A Positive Sense In The New Testament

If the Greek word epithumeo, translated as lust, is a word that means a sin, then surely the Holy Spirit would not have used the word in the following verses about angels, bishops, Jesus, the disciples, the prophets, and righteous men.

Here are some examples from the New Testament where the word for lust is used in a positive way. The words in bold are the English translation of the Greek word normally translated as lust in the New Testament.

> MATTHEW 13:17 KJV
> 17 For verily I say unto you, That many prophets and righteous men have **desired** to see those things which ye see, and have not seen them; and to hear those things which ye hear, and have not heard them.
>
> LUKE 17:22 KJV
> 22 And he said unto the disciples, The days will come, when ye shall **desire** to see one of the days of the Son of man, and ye shall not see it.
>
> LUKE 22:15 KJV
> 15 And he said unto them, With **desire** I have **desired** to eat this passover with you before I suffer:
>
> PHILIPPIANS 1:23 KJV
> 23 For I am in a strait betwixt two, having a **desire** to depart, and to be with Christ; which is far better:
>
> 1 THESSALONIANS 2:17 KJV
> 17 But we, brethren, being taken from you

for a short time in presence, not in heart, endeavoured the more abundantly to see your face with great **desire**.

1 TIMOTHY 3:1 KJV
1 This is a true saying, If a man desire the office of a bishop, he **desireth** a good work.

HEBREWS 6:11 KJV
11 And we **desire** that every one of you do shew the same diligence to the full assurance of hope unto the end:

1 PETER 1:12 KJV
12 Unto whom it was revealed, that not unto themselves, but unto us they did minister the things, which are now reported unto you by them that have preached the gospel unto you with the Holy Ghost sent down from heaven; which things the angels **desire** to look into.

Lust Is Used In A Positive Sense In The Old Testament

The following verses from the Old Testament contain the Hebrew word translated as "covet," (chamad), which is the word used in the 10th commandment in Exodus 20:17, making it the equivalent of the word translated as "lust" in the New Testament.

The words in bold are the English translation of the Hebrew word normally translated as covet in the Old Testament.

GENESIS 2:9 KJV
9 And out of the ground made the LORD God to grow every tree that is **pleasant** to the sight, and

good for food; the tree of life also in the midst of the garden, and the tree of knowledge of good and evil.

PSALM 19:8,10 KJV
8 The statutes of the LORD are right, rejoicing the heart: the commandment of the LORD is pure, enlightening the eyes.
10 More to be **desired** are they than gold, yea, than much fine gold: sweeter also than honey and the honeycomb.

PSALM 68:16 KJV
16 Why leap ye, ye high hills? this is the hill which God **desireth** to dwell in; yea, the LORD will dwell in it for ever.

PROVERBS 21:20 KJV
20 There is treasure to be **desired** and oil in the dwelling of the wise; but a foolish man spendeth it up.

SONG OF SOLOMON 2:3 KJV
3 As the apple tree among the trees of the wood, so is my beloved among the sons. I sat down under his shadow with great **delight**, and his fruit was sweet to my taste.

From all these verses above, you can see how this word translated "covet" was also used in a good sense. It was something the wise were to do and even God Himself did.

If you study the Bible closely, you will see that it is not always wrong to lust after something. For example the following verses from Deuteronomy have the word translated "lusteth" in the KJV, which is the Hebrew word "awah."

> DEUTERONOMY 12:15 KJV
> 15 Notwithstanding thou mayest kill and eat flesh in all thy gates, whatsoever thy soul **lusteth** after, according to the blessing of the LORD thy God which he hath given thee: the unclean and the clean may eat thereof, as of the roebuck, and as of the hart.
>
> DEUTERONOMY 12:20 KJV
> 20 When the LORD thy God shall enlarge thy border, as he hath promised thee, and thou shalt say, I will eat flesh, because thy soul longeth to eat flesh; thou mayest eat flesh, whatsoever thy soul **lusteth** after.
>
> DEUTERONOMY 14:26 KJV
> 26 And thou shalt bestow that money for whatsoever thy soul **lusteth** after, for oxen, or for sheep, or for wine, or for strong drink, or for whatsoever thy soul desireth: and thou shalt eat there before the LORD thy God, and thou shalt rejoice, thou, and thine household,
>
> DEUTERONOMY 14:26 CJB
> 26 and exchange the money for anything you want — cattle, sheep, wine, other intoxicating liquor, or anything you please — and you are to eat there in the presence of ADONAI your God, and enjoy yourselves, you and your household.

These verses indicate God desired for them and their families to enjoy themselves. God is not against us enjoying the good things of life, or of desiring them — even desiring them strongly (lusting after them). God is only against us "lusting after" what belongs to someone else and desiring to take them away from their rightful owners.

Not Just A Mental Sin

> ROMANS 13:9 KJV
> 9 For this, Thou shalt not commit adultery, Thou shalt not kill, Thou shalt not steal, Thou shalt not bear false witness, Thou shalt not covet; and if there be any other commandment, it is briefly comprehended in this saying, namely, Thou shalt love thy neighbour as thyself.

This verse makes it plain that the sin of coveting was something done against a human (neighbor). Because loving your neighbor includes all these commandments, therefore the Bible sin of coveting, which is the word also translated as lust (epithumeo), must be a sin against other people, not just some "inner sin" against God.

The New Testament, giving us a fuller revelation of God's will, tells us that divine love toward God and our neighbors is what God requires of us.

> ROMANS 13:10 NLT
> 10 Love does no wrong to others, so love fulfills the requirements of God's law.

I mention this because many people have the mistaken idea that "lust" or "coveting" is a mental sin against God. But the fact that the New Testament clearly tells us that the commandments — including "Do not covet" — are summed up in the command to love our neighbor, shows that "coveting" is a sin that would harm your neighbor. Thoughts alone do not harm a neighbor.

It is only when those thoughts are acted on and what belongs to your neighbor is taken from them that it is against the law of love.

> ROMANS 13:9 NLT
> 9 For the commandments say, "You must not commit adultery. You must not murder. You must not steal. You must not covet." These — and other such commandments — are summed up in this one commandment: "Love your neighbor as yourself."

Doctrine Of Devils

> 1 TIMOTHY 4:1 KJV
> 1 Now the Spirit speaketh expressly, that in the latter times some shall depart from the faith, giving heed to seducing spirits, and doctrines of devils;

The idea that "lust is a sin" is a doctrine of devils, who like to make people think God is unreasonable, which He would be if having sexual desire was a sin — since God is the One who created us with sexual desires.

To say that having sexual desire is a sin, when God created us so we could not avoid having such desires, is an insult to our Creator. Lust is why you are here. Without sexual desire on the part of your ancestors, you would never have been born.

It is true that sexual desire should be focused, and not allowed to control us. Sexual desire, like fire, is powerful, and productive, but must be kept under control. For if it gets out of control it can cause much harm.

Fire is not bad. Sexual desire (lust) is not bad. But they both must be kept under control. The Bible does teach self control.

Eating food is necessary for human survival. However, the Bible condemns gluttony. Sexual desire, or lust, is good, because God created it, but when it is allowed to run wild, it becomes wrong because it leads to sin.

But the devil has tried to sell us the lie that just having a sexual desire or a sexual thought is a sin. That is not true. It is only when we act on those thoughts and desires in ways the Bible tells us are wrong that it becomes a sin. The thought, no matter how evil, is not a sin, but only a temptation to sin.

> 1 TIMOTHY 4:1,3,4 NLT
> 1 Now the Holy Spirit tells us clearly that in the last times some will turn away from the true faith; they will follow deceptive spirits and teachings that come from demons.
> 3 They will say it is wrong to be married and wrong to eat certain foods. But God created those foods to be eaten with thanks by faithful people who know the truth.
> 4 Since everything God created is good, we should not reject any of it but receive it with thanks.

Everything God created is good. God created our human bodies and the hormones that cause us to have sexual desire. So sexual desire (or lust) is good. God created it and we should thank Him for it. It just needs to be controlled.

Flee Youthful Lusts

2 TIMOTHY 2:22 KJV
22 Flee also youthful lusts: but follow righteousness, faith, charity, peace, with them that call on the Lord out of a pure heart.

Many people automatically think of youthful lusts as sexual lusts, but that is not necessarily true. Flee youthful lusts, in the verse above, could be translated as flee childish desires. (And any older healthy person knows that sexual desire does not leave just because you are no longer a youth.)

William Hendriksen on page 273 of his *New Testament Commentary on Thessalonians, Timothy and Titus*[2] says of 2 Timothy 2:22, "it is wrong to construe the reference to be, either exclusively or predominantly, to uncontrolled sexual desire. The term, as here used, must probably be taken in its most general sense, as indicating any sinful yearning to which the soul of a young or relatively young person is exposed. In the present case there was, perhaps, the tendency of the younger man to be somewhat impatient with those who stood in the way. The sinful desires of youth may best be regarded in the most general sense, and thus as the antonyms of the virtues now mentioned: 'righteousness, faith, love, and peace.'"

Obviously, impatience is very prevalent in youth, and in the context makes more sense in this passage than sexual lusts. (Pride, rebellion, and selfishness are also usually found more often among the young.)

Don't Lust After Evil

> 1 CORINTHIANS 10:6 KJV
> 6 Now these things were our examples, to the intent we should not lust after evil things, as they also lusted.

It is still true that we should not lust after evil things. Obviously, that is a trap to avoid. So, we should not lust after anything God's Word tells us is wrong. It is wrong to lust after evil things, but it is not wrong to lust after good things that are God's will for us, as all the Scriptures above prove.

> 1 THESSALONIANS 4:3-7 NLT
> 3 God's will is for you to be holy, so stay away from all sexual sin.
> 4 Then each of you will control his own body and live in holiness and honor—
> 5 not in lustful passion like the pagans who do not know God and his ways.
> 6 Never harm or cheat a Christian brother in this matter by violating his wife, for the Lord avenges all such sins, as we have solemnly warned you before.
> 7 God has called us to live holy lives, not impure lives.

Most people think the Bible teaches that lust is always evil or bad. But when you analyze what the Bible really says, you find out that it is only lusting after evil or unlawful things that is wrong.

Sometimes the bias of the translators has crept in, making a verse seem like it is saying that lust is wrong. But we have proven above, using Scripture, that lust is not a sin, by itself. Since the Bible does not classify lust as a sin, we should not call lust a sin.

Lust is not a sin . . . but it can be dangerous. It is wise to avoid lust for wrong things. Because if we give place to the lust, it may overpower us and seize control of our will, and cause us to commit sin. But just having the lust is not a sin, by itself.

Thinking about sex or having sexual desires is not wrong in God's sight. Lust becomes wrong only when it takes control of us and gets us to act in a way clearly condemned in the Bible.

Chapter 5

"Lust After" Should Be Translated "Covet"

> MATTHEW 5:28 KJV
> 28 But I say unto you, That whosoever looketh on a woman to **lust after** her hath committed adultery with her already in his heart.

For Matthew 5:28 to have the same meaning to us as it did to the original hearers, the word translated as "lust after," which is the Greek word "epithumeo," should instead be translated as "covet."

In the Septuagint, the Scripture Jesus' hearers were familiar with, the tenth commandment began, "You shall not covet your neighbor's wife," and used the same word for "covet" that Jesus uses in Matthew 5:28 for "lust after," the Greek word "epithumeo." So everyone, as they heard Jesus speak this, would immediately have thought of the tenth commandment.

> EXODUS 20:17 LXE
> 17 Thou shalt not covet thy neighbour's wife; thou shalt not covet thy neighbour's house; nor his field, nor his servant, nor his maid, nor his ox, nor his ass, nor any of his cattle, nor whatever belongs to thy neighbour.

The Septuagint was the popular version of Scripture in Jesus' day, which was a Greek translation of the Old Testament. This was the primary "Bible" of the people Jesus was speaking to, and which they were very familiar with, just as most English-speaking Christians today are familiar with the wording of the King James translation of the Bible.

In the following three verses the King James version translates "epithumeo" as covet. Since the King James translators used the word covet to translate the Greek word "epithumeo" in these verses, you can see that my claim that it should also be translated as covet in Matthew 5:28 is not a wild idea.

> ACTS 20:33 KJV
> 33 I have **coveted** no man's silver, or gold, or apparel.
>
> ROMANS 13:9 KJV
> 9 For this, Thou shalt not commit adultery, Thou shalt not kill, Thou shalt not steal, Thou shalt not bear false witness, Thou shalt not **covet**; and if there be any other commandment, it is briefly comprehended in this saying, namely, Thou shalt love thy neighbour as thyself.
>
> ROMANS 7:7 KJV
> 7 What shall we say then? Is the law sin? God forbid. Nay, I had not known sin, but by the law: for I had not known **lust**, except the law had said, Thou shalt not **covet**.

Paul says in Romans 7:7 that ". . . I had not known lust (epithumia), except the law had said, Thou shalt not covet (epithumeo)." In this verse, the noun form of the Greek word, "epithumia" is translated as lust. The verb form of the same Greek word, "epithumeo" is translated as covet.

The point is that the KJV translators themselves translated the Greek word for "lust after," found in Matthew 5:28, as "covet" in other verses.

(As a note of explanation, Romans 7:7 does not say lust is a sin, but that without the aid of the Law, we would not have known what sin is. Coveting is a sin, and lust is better translated as covetousness here.)

What Does It Mean To Covet?

To covet is to desire to deprive another of his property, and that is the essence of adultery, as defined in the Bible: taking what belongs to another.

Lust, as it is popularly defined today, means strong sexual desire. But this is not necessarily what the word means when we find it in the Bible.

Just because lust in our culture means sexual desire and attraction, does not mean the Greek word translated as lust has that same meaning. As used here in Matthew 5:28, it means to desire to possess as one's own in a covetous way. It is the desire to steal what belongs to someone else.

To covet a married woman means to desire to take her for oneself. It would be desiring to break up the marriage so one could take another man's wife as his own. It is the intent to possess what belongs to another, and the strong desire to deprive another of his property by possessing it for yourself.

Covetousness is a motivation behind theft. If that desire to steal another's property is not present, then it is not Biblical covetousness (which is here translated as lust).

So, in Matthew 5:28, Jesus is talking about a man who looks at a married woman with the desire and intention to take her away from her husband. Without that intention to deprive a man of his wife and take her for one's own, there is no adultery involved in looking, even if he looks at a married woman with sexual desire, appreciation, and enjoyment.

L. William Countryman, in his book, *Dirt Greed & Sex, Sexual Ethics in the New Testament and Their Implications For Today*[1] says on pages 177-178, "In this case, Matthew has Jesus saying that covetousness, the desire to deprive another of his property, is the essence of adultery. Jesus was then reaffirming a quite traditional understanding of what is wrong in adultery. In this case, however, Jesus was asserting that adultery does not consist primarily in the sexual union of two people at least one of whom is "one flesh" with another person; it consists rather in the intention, accomplished or not, to take what belongs to another."

Looking at a woman, married or not, with fascination, appreciation, or even sexual excitement is not what Jesus was referring to in Matthew 5:28, but rather to the desire to take her away from someone else.

So we can, and should, translate Matthew 5:28: But I say unto you, that whosoever looketh on a wife to covet her, that is to desire to take her away from her husband for oneself, hath committed adultery with her already in his heart.

Chapter 6

What Is Sin?

A sin is a selfish act that harms someone.

This view of sin may be new to you, but it explains sin in accordance with all of Scripture in a way we can easily understand.

After you read this, you will understand sin. And you will see that God has set up judgment on a basis that will be clear and accepted as right by all. All people will readily agree that sin is bad, once they understand what sin is.

The word "sin" in the New Testament is a translation of the Greek word "hamartia," which means to miss the mark. So, sin is falling short of God's standard, missing the mark set by God.

> ROMANS 3:23 NLT
> 23 For everyone has sinned; we all fall short of God's glorious standard.

The mark, or the standard by which we measure, is God Himself, and His nature of giving love. When we act in selfish ways, disregarding the feelings and welfare of all others, we fall short of what God desires and expects from people who were made in His image and likeness.

A sin is a selfish act done at someone's expense. Another way to say it would be "acts done intentionally that result in harm or loss to someone."

Not all selfish acts are sin, just because they are selfish. (I define "selfish" here as being concerned exclusively with oneself.) Only when the act is done at the expense of another person, or causes them harm, does it become a sin. For example, it is a selfish act to drink water and eat food, because it is solely for our benefit, but it is not a sin, unless you take that water or food away from someone, or refuse to share it with those around you, if they are in need of it.

Good News For Sinners

Before we go any further, it is important to point out — no matter how you define sin — Jesus paid the penalty for your sins. By receiving Jesus Christ you also receive forgiveness for all your sins. So, no matter what sin is, you have the solution in receiving Jesus Christ.

> COLOSSIANS 1:14 GWN
> 14 His Son paid the price to free us, which means that our sins are forgiven.

> 2 CORINTHIANS 5:19 NLT
> 19 For God was in Christ, reconciling the world to himself, no longer counting people's sins against them. And he gave us this wonderful message of reconciliation.

The only sin that would ultimately condemn someone is to reject God's love by rejecting Jesus Christ, His free gift to you.

> JOHN 16:9 NLT
> 9 The world's sin is that it refuses to believe in me.

Jesus Christ is our only way out of this mess. There is no other Savior. Without Jesus we are helpless, hopeless, and lost.

> ACTS 4:12 NLT
> 12 There is salvation in no one else! God has given no other name under heaven by which we must be saved."

Fortunately, Jesus is the friend of sinners, and He will receive anyone who comes to Him. We don't have to be perfect for Jesus to receive us. We just have to turn to Him and ask Him into our life. (To learn more, read *Even If You Have Sinned, You Can Be Forgiven,* starting on page 85.)

Teachers Can Be Wrong

Not everything that people think of as a sin, is really a sin according to the Bible.

Religious tradition labels many things as sin which the Bible does not. People make up all kinds of rules based on what they think is right. But God is the judge and only God can tell us what sin is.

No matter how much you may respect your pastor or priest or teacher, they are not the final authority. All humans can be wrong.

> MARK 7:9 KJV
> 9 And he said unto them, Full well ye reject the commandment of God, that ye may keep your own tradition.

God has not left us to wonder what sin is. We don't have to guess, or make it up as we go. The Bible reveals to us what sin is.

Just because you do something someone else thinks is wrong, does not mean it is a sin. So don't let people condemn you over things the Bible does not clearly say are wrong.

Looking For A Definition For Sin

How do we know what sin is? God reveals to us in the Bible what is a sin, and therefore, we can also know what is not a sin.

What does the New Testament actually say about sin?

> 1 JOHN 3:4 KJV
> 4 Whosoever committeth sin transgresseth also the law: for sin is the transgression of the law.

At first it seems that 1 John 3:4 has made it simple for us, defining sin as "the transgression of the Law." But further study reveals that this translation may not be accurate. In reality, it is probably telling us that "lawlessness is sin," which is a quite different statement, having a much more restricted meaning. It is like the difference between saying "adultery is sin," and saying "sin is adultery." Certainly, adultery is sin, but there are more sins than just adultery, and there are also more sins mentioned in Scripture than just being a lawless person.

Proof that the apparent definition of sin in 1 John 3:4 is not comprehensive, comes from the statement in Romans 5:13 that there is sin apart from the Old Testament Law.

What Is Sin?

> ROMANS 5:13 NLT
> 13 Yes, people sinned even before the law was given. But it was not counted as sin because there was not yet any law to break.

Before the giving of God's Law, because there was no law to break, sins were not counted against people. But from God's viewpoint, people were still sinning before the Law was given. This shows us sin has to be something besides breaking the Law.

Further clues that the apparent definition of sin in 1 John 3:4 may not be comprehensive, are the verses telling us that whatever is not done in faith is sin, and that it is sin if you know to do something, yet fail to do it. Neither of these actions, which are called sin, require directly breaking the Law. We will explain both of these verses later, showing how our definition of sin is comprehensive, fitting all the Scripture on the subject of sin.

> JAMES 4:17 KJV
> 17 Therefore to him that knoweth to do good, and doeth it not, to him it is sin.

> ROMANS 14:23 NLT
> 23 But if you have doubts about whether or not you should eat something, you are sinning if you go ahead and do it. For you are not following your convictions. If you do anything you believe is not right, you are sinning.

Temptations Are Not Sins

Another error is thinking temptation is a sin. Temptation itself is not sin. You cannot help being tempted. Even Jesus was tempted — but He never yielded to sin.

> HEBREWS 4:15 NIV
> 15 For we do not have a high priest who is unable to sympathize with our weaknesses, but we have one who has been tempted in every way, just as we are — yet was without sin.

Temptations are not sins. Lust (a strong desire) must "conceive," and bring forth sinful action, for there to be a sin.

> JAMES 1:14-15 KJV
> 14 But every man is tempted, when he is drawn away of his own lust, and enticed.
> 15 Then when lust hath conceived, it bringeth forth sin: and sin, when it is finished, bringeth forth death.

Only after "lust hath conceived" does it bring forth sin. So, temptation, or lust, by itself is not sin.

A common mistake is believing that having bad thoughts is a sin. It is not a sin to be tempted with bad thoughts. It only becomes a sin when we embrace those thoughts as our own and decide to act on them.

Sin Harms People

The reason God is against sin is because He loves people. God desires the best for all people, but sin keeps that from happening.

> JAMES 1:15 NLT
> 15 These desires give birth to sinful actions. And when sin is allowed to grow, it gives birth to death.

God is against sin because it is deadly. Sin brings forth death, not life and blessing. God loves people, so He is against everything that harms people.

All sin harms someone. (Just because you don't see how a sin would harm anyone, does not mean you know more than God.) There is no sin that does not hurt someone — either you, someone you are sinning against, or God.

> ROMANS 6:23 KJV
> 23 For the wages of sin is death; but the gift of God is eternal life through Jesus Christ our Lord.

The trouble is that sin is a real killer. Sin pays wages of death. That is why God is against sin, because God is for people.

God Is Not Bossy

God takes no delight in ordering people around. He has no need to prop up His self-esteem by forcing us to obey Him.

God did not give us His Word because He wants to throw His weight around and give orders. God's commands and instructions are not oppressive, but they are given because God loves us and desires to help us.

Many Christian teachers would say that sin is disobeying God's command. But sin is more than just breaking a command from on high. God did not give us arbitrary, or frivolous commands. Sin is an objective fact, not just disobeying an order from on high. Sin is a reality of evil everyone can easily recognize as dangerous, once we have our eyes opened to the truth.

> 1 JOHN 4:8 KJV
> 8 He that loveth not knoweth not God; for God is love.

God is love. That means His very nature is one that puts the interests and welfare of others ahead of His own. So any command God has ever given has been given for the benefit of mankind, not for any other reason.

Let me state it again: God does not give commands for His own benefit, but for humanity's benefit.

People who rebel and go any other way than God's way are hurt by their actions, because His way is perfect. Any other way will eventually harm us, or others. That is why something is a sin, not just because God said it is wrong. God only tells us what is wrong, so we can avoid the pain it brings.

How Do We Sin Against God?

Sin can be done against other people, against God, or even against yourself.

Whenever you disobey God you sin against God, because of your lack of respect for Him, and you also sin against yourself. The reason is that God's will is perfect, so doing anything other than God's will is harmful to your best interest.

How is sin against God a selfish act done at His expense?

God is a great being who has never done wrong. He is perfect, having never committed a selfish act done at the expense of another. All His actions have been done in love, in the best interest of all concerned. Because of this perfect record, God has earned our respect, honor, and love.

A parent who sacrifices and provides for a child for 20 years deserves some respect from that child for all they have done for them. God is the ultimate, perfect parent. He has done infinitely more for us than any earthly parent, and also deserves our respect.

In the beginning, before man's disobedience and fall, God created us and gave us a beautiful world filled with all the good things we would need or enjoy. He showered His love and blessing on us, giving us richly all things to enjoy.

When we fail to love God, honor Him, and respect Him in return, we rob Him of what He deserves and cause Him pain. We hurt God by our callous, unthankful, disrespectful response. When we refuse to believe God, who cannot lie, and never has lied, we question His integrity. It is no different than slapping Him in the face.

These actions, because they hurt God and cause Him pain, are selfish actions done at God's expense. So they are sin.

Some people may think God is beyond being hurt or offended, but the following verses show differently.

> GENESIS 6:6 NIV
> 6 The LORD was grieved that he had made man on the earth, and his heart was filled with pain.
>
> EPHESIANS 4:30 KJV
> 30 And grieve not the holy Spirit of God, whereby ye are sealed unto the day of redemption.

God has feelings, just like you do. God is a Person. He does not enjoy being ignored, neglected, or disrespected any more than you do.

Whatever Is Not Done In Faith

ROMANS 14:23 KJV
23 And he that doubteth is damned if he eat, because he eateth not of faith: for whatsoever is not of faith is sin.

Why is "whatsoever is not of faith" a sin?

If you believe something you are doing is a sin, then for you to do it requires an act of rebellion, a conscious decision on your part to do something you believe a loving, wise, and perfect Father God declared is wrong. When you do that, you are a rebel, obviously showing no respect or concern for what God thinks and says about the matter.

Consider the matter of drinking coffee or soda pop. God never said in the Bible that drinking them was a sin. Personally, I don't think these beverages are good for you. But that does not make drinking them a sin. However, if you believe it is wrong for you to drink them — yet you do — then it is a sin for you, because you would then be doing it out of rebellion. Since you believe it is wrong, every time you do it you are making a conscious decision to act in a way that you know (or at least you think you know) is against God's will. That is an act of rebellion against God's love.

ROMANS 14:23 NLT
23 But if you have doubts about whether or not you should eat something, you are sinning if you go ahead and do it. For you are not following

your convictions. If you do anything you believe is not right, you are sinning.

God has earned our respect, admiration, and honor, and it rightly belongs to Him because He has earned it. He has been faithful to His own nature of selfless love and putting the interests of others first for all of history. There is no record or evidence that God, or His human incarnation Jesus Christ, has ever committed a selfish act of sin.

Not Doing Good When You Should

JAMES 4:17 CJB
17 So then, anyone who knows the right thing to do and fails to do it is committing a sin.

If you know something is the right thing to do, then doing something else is willfully making a decision to do wrong. At the very least you are sinning against yourself, and probably against others also.

Ignoring the needs of others when you are there and have the means to help them is obviously a selfish action that causes others harm. This should really need no explanation.

The New Commandment

In the New Testament, Jesus gave us a command which summarizes all the commands of the Old Covenant that we need to keep. That command is to love as He loved.

GALATIANS 5:14 NET
14 For the whole law can be summed up in a single commandment, namely, "You must love your neighbor as yourself."

Any step out of divine love is sin because it disobeys Christ's new commandment to love others even as He loved us.

> JOHN 13:34-35 KJV
> 34 A new commandment I give unto you, That ye love one another; as I have loved you, that ye also love one another.
> 35 By this shall all men know that ye are my disciples, if ye have love one to another.

This divine love, that Jesus said would be a mark of His followers, is the opposite of selfishness.

Why is it that Jesus' true disciples are distinguished by their love shown to others? Because without being born again and receiving the life and nature of God in our heart, it is impossible to love others as much as we love ourselves. Unless we are born again, we are slaves of sin, caught in a vicious cycle of selfishness that continues to harm us and harm others. Once we receive Jesus, we are set free from this bondage and have the capacity to love as He loved. No human who is not born again has the capacity to demonstrate divine love.

> JOHN 15:12 KJV
> 12 This is my commandment, That ye love one another, as I have loved you.

The law of love goes much further than most people have realized. It means to put the interests of others first. It means to do what is in the best interest of everyone. It doesn't mean just having a "feeling of love."

> EPHESIANS 5:33 KJV
> 33 Nevertheless let every one of you in particular

so love his wife even as himself; and the wife see that she reverence her husband.

We should not think the meaning of Jesus' commandment to love is a light one. It involves not just some feeling, but actions that put the interests of others first. Jesus demonstrated it by going so far as death to help others.

> JOHN 15:13 KJV
> 13 Greater love hath no man than this, that a man lay down his life for his friends.

Divine love means being willing to suffer rather than to see someone else suffer harm. This is the kind of love Jesus demonstrated, and the kind of love we are to show to the world.

We may know that we should love others. But without God's revelation we cannot realize the full long-term ramifications of our actions, and thus judge accurately what is truly love toward others. We don't have the benefit of centuries of personal experience to know what our actions will ultimately produce.

For example, consider the subject of having sex with a young single woman. Even if she wants to have sex with you, the question to ask is, "Would it be in her best long-term interest?"

Are you taking into account her emotions, her expectations, and what is best for her long-term happiness and welfare? If you are just using her for temporary entertainment, how can that be in her best interest?

Do you really think she will be better off for her whole life, because you used her for sex for a while, and then abandoned her? Are you taking into consideration what would happen if she became pregnant or got a sexually transmitted disease from your sexual encounter?

If it is not in your best interest, her best interest, and the best interest of society as a whole, then it is not a loving action, but a selfish action, and therefore sinful. It may be selfish on your part and her part, too. Both of you could want to do it, yet be harming others by your selfish action.

How can a young person know the hurt and pain that can be caused by having a "casual" sexual encounter just one time? How can they know the generations of misery that can result from that one act done in the heat of passion? They certainly can't know from their own experience, so God spelled it out in the Bible, so we could avoid the pain of having to learn on our own.

Living by the Law of Love, while simple to state, is much more complicated to practice, because it involves seeing things from the perspective of others and determining what would be in their best interest.

To love everyone means you desire the best for everyone, and are willing to act accordingly. It does not mean you have to like everyone, or approve of all they do. It just means you desire to help people, not harm them.

Why didn't God just start out telling people the love commandment, instead of giving all the Old Testament laws first? It could be because the love commandment seems so simple on the surface that most people would miss it by not understanding its depth. We humans do not have the experience God has, so we don't know the outcome of many actions. We have not personally viewed them in operation like God has many times over the years. But once we have our eyes opened by God's revelation, we can understand why sin is wrong. With God's help, we can then apply the law of love to every situation, determining what is in the best interest of all involved, including society around us and our descendants yet unborn.

Take Another Look At Selfishness

No one ever sins for another person. You may sin because of another person, to impress them or influence them, but no one ever sins for someone else. All sin is selfish.

Selfishness is the essence of sin. It is why sin existed even before the Law was given. People were selfish and self-centered, but they didn't realize how bad they were until the Law was given.

Selfishness is a focus on yourself: what you think and what you want. It is going your own way instead of God's way. Selfishness is ultimately rebellion against God, because it puts "self" ahead of everything and everyone else.

Pride is the root of selfishness, thinking you know more than God, or that you are a better judge of what should be done than God. That will cause you to rebel against God's way and sin.

Compared to God, who is love — selfish people are detestable. Who would want to live for eternity with a bunch of self-centered, selfish brats who cared only for their own interests?

Not me! And obviously, not God either!

Think about it: the only thing necessary to turn Heaven into Hell would be to allow selfishness there.

The root, or cause, of all sin is selfishness. The reason people murder someone is essentially selfishness. The one they murder is somehow a roadblock to their perceived happiness. So, you can never fully trust someone who is selfish.

Loving other people, and loving God, is the opposite of acting in selfishness.

> 1 JOHN 3:14-16 NLT
> 14 If we love our Christian brothers and sisters, it proves that we have passed from death to life. But a person who has no love is still dead.
> 15 Anyone who hates another brother or sister is really a murderer at heart. And you know that murderers don't have eternal life within them.
> 16 We know what real love is because Jesus gave up his life for us. So we also ought to give up our lives for our brothers and sisters.

Eternal life enables people to overcome selfishness because God's love is deposited in our hearts when we are born again. We still must choose to walk in love, but with eternal life in our hearts, we have the ability to walk in God's divine love.

> PHILIPPIANS 2:3-4 NET
> 3 Instead of being motivated by selfish ambition or vanity, each of you should, in humility, be moved to treat one another as more important than yourself.
> 4 Each of you should be concerned not only about your own interests, but about the interests of others as well.

Caring only about your interests, with no regard for the interests of others, is wrong. It is not wrong to love yourself, only to love yourself at the expense of others. We are to love our neighbors as we love our selves. It only becomes wrong when we do something to benefit ourselves and it harms our neighbor.

We Have A New Covenant

We are now dead to the ceremonial laws of the Old Testament Law through the death of Christ as our substitute. These ceremonial laws were just a shadow and symbolic to point us to Christ. Those demands of the Jewish Law no longer have any jurisdiction over us. Instead we are to live by the new commandment given by Jesus to love one another.

Under the New Covenant, we are not just supposed to follow a list of rules. We are to be born again, receiving the life and nature of God in our inner beings, changing our heart, and giving us the ability to walk in love instead of living in selfishness.

This is God's answer for the sin problem: giving us His nature of love so we won't desire to continue to do selfish acts at the expense of others.

God not only set us an example by His love action, but gave us His life and nature, so it would be natural for us to also act in divine love, always seeking what is best for others.

This is why the Bible says that someone who is born of God does not continue to practice sin. Sure, we can slip, but it is no longer our nature to be selfish and desire to take advantage of others and do them wrong.

    1 JOHN 3:9 NLT
    9 Those who have been born into God's family

do not make a practice of sinning, because God's life is in them. So they can't keep on sinning, because they are children of God.

You may say that there are Christians who still are very selfish in their actions and seem to have no regard for the interest and welfare of others. These people are not living and acting out of their inner nature, but out of their unrenewed minds. They need to grow spiritually, and allow the fruit of the spirit to grow and be manifest in their life.

Or, they may not be born again. Many people are just members of some church or religious group, but have never truly received God's gift of eternal life, which comes when we truly receive Jesus Christ. They may be just church members, not true children of God.

Are There Mental Sins?

Are there sins which are just in the mental realm? No. Only actions are sins. There is no such thing as a sin which is just a mental sin, a thought. Thoughts can lead to sin, but thoughts are not sin, in and of themselves: not unless they bring forth some type of action.

For it to become sin, it has to involve your will. You have to make a decision, which is an action. After you make the decision to sin, it is only a matter of time and opportunity until the sinful action is completed. Making a decision is the first action step on the path of sin. Until a decision is made, the thought of sin has not taken any control of you. A decision is the first step in bringing forth a sin.

> MATTHEW 15:19 KJV
> 19 For out of the heart proceed evil thoughts,

murders, adulteries, fornications, thefts, false witness, blasphemies:

Sin proceeds from, or originates in, the human heart, not the human mind, and must have the approval of the human will.

In Greek, as in English, there is a different word for heart and mind. "Heart" means the core of your being, who you really are, and thus refers in Scripture to the human spirit, which is also the part of you that is "born again" when you receive Jesus Christ and become a Christian.

Expressing an attitude is an action. Showing an attitude of resentment, or of hate, is an action.

Expressing disappointment over your wife's body because you have been viewing pornography and dwelling on how she falls short in your estimation, is a sin. Expressing these negative feelings in a way that hurts your wife is an action and a sin. It was a selfish action done by you at her expense, which harmed her.

This is why it is best to avoid most lust. Lust is not a sin, but if you welcome it and incubate it, most likely it will be expressed eventually in your actions.

> MATTHEW 12:34-37 CJB
> 34 You snakes! How can you who are evil say anything good? For the mouth speaks what overflows from the heart.
> 35 The good person brings forth good things from his store of good, and the evil person brings forth evil things from his store of evil.
> 36 Moreover, I tell you this: on the Day of Judgment people will have to give account for

every careless word they have spoken;
37 for by your own words you will be acquitted, and by your own words you will be condemned."

Why will people have to face judgment for every careless word they have spoken? Because every careless word was an action that hurt someone. Words are the primary way humans express themselves. The thought of hate or unfaithfulness is not a sin. But it becomes a sin when we speak words expressing those things from our heart.

People will not be judged by their thoughts, but by their words, which are actions, and by their other actions, also. Thoughts are not sin. They only lead to sin.

Understanding this should not encourage you to dwell on bad thoughts, which is dangerous, as those thoughts can seize you and lead you to sin. Bad thoughts should not be welcomed and entertained. But it is important to realize that bad thoughts — no matter how evil they are — are not sins. So we can resist the devil's lies telling us we have sinned just because we had a bad thought.

This is the devil's strategy: to encourage bad thoughts and then accuse us of sin, so we will grow discouraged and feel we can never overcome sin. But it is a lie. Thoughts are not sin.

Don't Be Discouraged

Through our study we have found that all selfish acts that harm others are sin. And every one of us is guilty. There is not one person on earth who has not sinned. We all need God's mercy, forgiveness, and help. (You may also have realized that some things you have been taught were sin, are not sins, according to the true teaching of the Bible.)

Thank God we can be forgiven! So there is hope and help for everyone, no matter how badly you have sinned.

God loves all people, so He conceived a plan to forgive us, bring us into His family, and cause us to grow up to be like Him — people who love others.

When we receive Jesus Christ, we receive His nature of love in our innermost heart, enabling us to love others as Jesus loves them, instead of sinning against them. But it is also true that we continue living in the same bodies that have been trained in sin, and have the same mindset, as before we received Jesus. So, although our hearts are new and desire to do what is right, we can still face struggles because we still have the same body and mind as we did before receiving Jesus.

We need to read and study the Bible to cause our minds to be renewed, so we can think in line with God. And we must retrain our bodies to have good habits, instead of our previous bad habits. For some people this seems to happen more easily and quickly than for others. Regardless of how slow your spiritual progress may seem, you need to know that God is patient. He is here to help you, not to condemn you. Jesus already suffered the penalty your sins deserve, so you can now go free.

When we are born again, we receive the ability to overcome all sin, but we must grow into it, just like a newborn human child must grow and develop to exhibit his full potential. A child is born with all the muscles he will ever have, but those muscles must be used and developed before the child can become an Olympic athlete.

So, please don't become discouraged if it seems like it is difficult for you to quit sinning, even though inwardly you desire to do so. It may take some time to change your habits and grow spiritually, but God will help you.

Every time you sin, don't run from God, but run to Him and receive forgiveness. It doesn't matter if you do the same sin over and over, God will never refuse to forgive you, because Jesus has paid the penalty for all sin. The reality is that God has already forgiven us. We just need to come to God to receive His forgiveness, which has been already given to us, so we can benefit from it.

> 1 JOHN 1:9 NLT
> 9 But if we confess our sins to him, he is faithful and just to forgive us our sins and to cleanse us from all wickedness.

God will never turn His back on you, regardless of how much you sin. God loves you, but sin keeps you from having God's best in your life, so you need to turn away from sin with God's help.

God won't give up on you, so keep trusting in Him no matter how much you fail. God is for you, not against you. Just as a good father will help his child, God will help you, if you will let Him.

> PSALM 103:8-14 NLT
> 8 The LORD is compassionate and merciful, slow to get angry and filled with unfailing love.
> 9 He will not constantly accuse us, nor remain angry forever.
> 10 He does not punish us for all our sins; he does not deal harshly with us, as we deserve.
> 11 For his unfailing love toward those who fear him is as great as the height of the heavens

above the earth.
12 He has removed our sins as far from us as the east is from the west.
13 The LORD is like a father to his children, tender and compassionate to those who fear him.
14 For he knows how weak we are; he remembers we are only dust.

God desires for you to be in His family, enjoying His love and blessing, starting now and lasting through all eternity. Therefore, God took care of the sin problem which would separate you from Him, by sending Jesus to die in your place. Make sure you take advantage of God's provision, so you can enjoy His blessing. Receive Jesus Christ, and receive God's forgiveness now!

"Lord Jesus, I receive You now as my Lord and Savior. Thank You for forgiving me of all my sins, and giving me Your love nature in my heart. Please continue to work Your will in my life to make it what it should be."

Chapter 7

Conclusion: Looking At Women Is Not A Sin

MATTHEW 5:28 KJV
28 But I say unto you, That whosoever looketh on a woman to lust after her hath committed adultery with her already in his heart.

People who read Matthew 5:28 in any widely-used English translation think Jesus said it was wrong to look at a woman and be sexually attracted to her. Many think Jesus said that looking with lust at a woman is just as bad as committing adultery by having sexual intercourse.

But Jesus did not say that. Neither did Jesus mean that.

The New Testament was originally written in the Greek language, and all English versions are translations from the Greek. Translation is never an exact science, so sometimes the bias of a translator can creep in, and we have to dig deeper and study to get the original meaning.

Our misunderstanding of this verse is due to a difference in our cultures, causing us to have translations which fail to communicate the same truth to us today, as it did to the original hearers.

We have shown that the word translated as "woman" should be translated as "wife." This is the only possible meaning the people Jesus was speaking to could have given to the word He used in this verse.

Why?

Because of how the people Jesus was speaking to viewed adultery. From our study of the Old Testament teaching on adultery, we realize it is different from our modern viewpoint.

Today, in our culture, adultery is sexual intercourse by any person outside their marriage. Although this may be a good definition, it is not what the people who heard Jesus speak these words originally would have understood by His use of the word "adultery."

The Bible Meaning Of Adultery

According to the usage of the word adultery in the Bible, a man, whether married or single, can only commit adultery with another man's wife. If a married man had a sexual relationship with an unmarried woman, it was not considered adultery.

So the people Jesus spoke to would never think of the possibility of adultery unless a married woman was involved. This is why the Greek word "gyne" in Matthew 5:28 must be translated as wife (instead of woman), as that is the only possible meaning those who heard Jesus could have attached to it.

Once you understand this word must be translated as "wife," not "woman," it becomes clear Jesus could not

Conclusion: Looking At Women Is Not A Sin

have meant what the English translations seem to say. For we would not know if a woman is married or not, just by glancing at her. And to commit whatever sin Jesus was talking about, a married wife would have to be involved, not just any woman.

Jesus was not introducing a new definition of adultery. He was just telling us the sin starts at the point when we make the decision and start planning to commit the act. In God's sight you are guilty as soon as you decide to commit the sin. Not just if you commit the act and get caught.

"Lust After" Should Be Translated "Covet"

We have found another key in understanding the word translated as "lust after" in Matthew 5:28.

The Greek word translated as "lust" means a strong desire. It does not have to be sexual in nature. Scripture applies this word to angels, bishops, Jesus, the disciples, the prophets, and righteous men, so it is not necessarily a sin. It just means a strong desire. In fact, as we discovered in our study, lust is not a sin, but only a temptation that can lead us to sin.

In Matthew 5:28 the word translated "lust" is translated as "covet" in the Greek Old Testament which was used in Jesus' day (the Septuagint translation). This word was used in the tenth commandment, in Exodus 20:17.

> EXODUS 20:17 KJV
> 17 Thou shalt not covet thy neighbour's house, thou shalt not covet thy neighbour's wife, nor his manservant, nor his maidservant, nor

his ox, nor his ass, nor any thing that is thy neighbour's.

This tenth commandment is not one that humans can judge or enforce. But the Law still says it is wrong. Jesus was not instituting a new commandment about adultery or coveting, but merely stating what the tenth commandment already said, that it is a sin to desire to deprive another man of his property.

Even if you do not break the letter of the other commandments, but you want to do so in your heart, and make the decision to commit the sin, you are guilty. God judges a sinful heart, and hearts that covet what belongs to others, and make the decision to take it from them, are guilty.

So, in Matthew 5:28, Jesus was saying that covetousness, which is the desire to deprive another of his property, is the essence of adultery. Jesus was reaffirming a quite traditional understanding of adultery with those who heard him.

Jesus was not condemning looking at the property of another man with admiration, but He was condemning deciding to take another man's property from him.

(It is not my thinking that a wife should be considered property. But that was the general mindset of the time when the commandment was given, and during Jesus' earthly ministry.)

What Is Sin?

Sin is missing the mark set by God. A sin is a selfish act that harms someone. Thoughts are not sin. Thoughts are only temptations that try to lead us to sin.

Conclusion: Looking At Women Is Not A Sin

Religious tradition labels many things as sin which the Bible does not. People make up all kinds of rules based on what they think is right. But God is the judge and only God is qualified to tell us what sin is.

It is not a sin to look at women, no matter how long you look, or how much you may enjoy looking, whether they are married or unmarried. But if, while you continue looking at a married woman, you are also planning how to seduce her, clearly you have now made the decision, and all you lack is the opportunity to fulfil the act. So, you are guilty of adultery because you have the intent to commit adultery — you already made the decision to commit adultery in your heart.

From what Jesus said we can understand that when you make the decision to sin, you are guilty of sin at that point, because you have already started on the path of wrong action.

Please keep in mind that hurting someone (such as your wife) by your actions, is wrong. (Based on Jesus' commandment to love others.) We should not use our freedom to "enjoy the view God created" in a way that harms our wife. God never told us it is wrong to look at women, but He did tell us to love our wife.

Since the law of God never told us it was a sin to look at a woman, as long as no one is harmed by it, then it cannot be a sin. It has only been a religious misunderstanding of what Jesus said that caused it to be falsely labeled as a sin, which it is not, according to the correct interpretation of the Bible.

Even If You Have Sinned, You Can Be Forgiven

In this book we have proven that just looking at women is not a sin.

But if you have crossed the line and committed acts that you know are sins, you have opened the door for big trouble. Sin hurts people. That is why God is against sin, because He loves people.

The good news is, whether you are a Christian believer, or not, you can receive forgiveness for all your sins today.

If you have sinned as a Christian, the Bible is clear on what you should do, and what the Lord will do.

> 1 JOHN 1:9 NLT
> 9 But if we confess our sins to him, he is faithful and just to forgive us our sins and to cleanse us from all wickedness.

God has already provided for forgiveness of all sins — for all people — through the sacrifice of Jesus. We do not have to convince God to forgive us. It was His idea. All we have to do is agree with God that we did sin, and receive His forgiveness. God has already declared that forgiveness is ours, we just have to come to Him by faith, trusting His Word, and receive it.

The Bible places no limits, or restrictions, on how often we can be forgiven. In fact, Jesus indicated we should forgive others in an unlimited manner, so we know God would not do any less than He asks of us.

> MATTHEW 18:21-22 NLT
> 21 Then Peter came to him and asked, "Lord, how often should I forgive someone who sins against me? Seven times?"
> 22 "No, not seven times," Jesus replied, "but seventy times seven!

All human beings have sinned. We have all fallen short and need a Savior. It is only by God's grace and His forgiveness that anyone can be right with God.

> ROMANS 6:23 NLT
> 23 For the wages of sin is death, but the free gift of God is eternal life through Christ Jesus our Lord.

We can be glad because Jesus Christ came to save sinners, and He paid the price for the forgiveness of all sins by shedding His blood. No matter how badly you have sinned, you can receive forgiveness today. In fact, God has already forgiven you. He is just waiting on you to come to Him and receive that forgiveness, so you can be in right standing with Him as a free gift. This is Good News because sin produces death and we all need a Savior.

> ROMANS 5:17 NLT
> 17 For the sin of this one man, Adam, caused death to rule over many. But even greater

is God's wonderful grace and his gift of righteousness, for all who receive it will live in triumph over sin and death through this one man, Jesus Christ.

Jesus paid the price in full for your complete forgiveness and cleansing from all sin — no matter what you have done. You can be done with it and put it in the past today. Not only can you be forgiven of all your sins, but God will work in you to change you and enable you to overcome those sins that have trapped you in the past. With God's help you can overcome! You can be free from the power of sin to control you!

> ROMANS 3:19-28 NLT
> 19 Obviously, the law applies to those to whom it was given, for its purpose is to keep people from having excuses, and to show that the entire world is guilty before God.
> 20 For no one can ever be made right with God by doing what the law commands. The law simply shows us how sinful we are.
> 21 But now God has shown us a way to be made right with him without keeping the requirements of the law, as was promised in the writings of Moses and the prophets long ago.
> 22 We are made right with God by placing our faith in Jesus Christ. And this is true for everyone who believes, no matter who we are.
> 23 For everyone has sinned; we all fall short of God's glorious standard.
> 24 Yet God, with undeserved kindness, declares that we are righteous. He did this through Christ Jesus when he freed us from the penalty for our sins.
> 25 For God presented Jesus as the sacrifice for

sin. People are made right with God when they believe that Jesus sacrificed his life, shedding his blood. This sacrifice shows that God was being fair when he held back and did not punish those who sinned in times past,
26 for he was looking ahead and including them in what he would do in this present time. God did this to demonstrate his righteousness, for he himself is fair and just, and he declares sinners to be right in his sight when they believe in Jesus.
27 Can we boast, then, that we have done anything to be accepted by God? No, because our acquittal is not based on obeying the law. It is based on faith.
28 So we are made right with God through faith and not by obeying the law.

ROMANS 5:6-11 NLT
6 When we were utterly helpless, Christ came at just the right time and died for us sinners.
7 Now, most people would not be willing to die for an upright person, though someone might perhaps be willing to die for a person who is especially good.
8 But God showed his great love for us by sending Christ to die for us while we were still sinners.
9 And since we have been made right in God's sight by the blood of Christ, he will certainly save us from God's condemnation.
10 For since our friendship with God was restored by the death of his Son while we were still his enemies, we will certainly be saved through the life of his Son.

11 So now we can rejoice in our wonderful new relationship with God because our Lord Jesus Christ has made us friends of God.

ROMANS 10:9-10 NLT
9 If you confess with your mouth that Jesus is Lord and believe in your heart that God raised him from the dead, you will be saved.
10 For it is by believing in your heart that you are made right with God, and it is by confessing with your mouth that you are saved.

JOHN 1:12 NLT
12 But to all who believed him and accepted him, he gave the right to become children of God.

Jesus is the friend of sinners, and He will receive anyone who comes to Him. You don't have to be perfect for Jesus to receive you. You just have to receive Him. Then He will save you and make you a child of God.

As Romans 10:9-10 reveals, speaking words, declaring that you put your trust in Jesus Christ and receive Him as Lord, is how you receive Jesus. In that sense, it is similar to getting married: you say "I do" and you make it publicly known.

If you have made this decision, please let us know through the web site: www.LookingAtWomenIsNotASin.com

Why I Am Selling This Book

Why am I selling this book, instead of just making it all available free on the Internet?

One reason: I believe the Lord Jesus led me to do it this way. I think the reasons He did all add up to more people reading it and being set free by its message, and as a result of that, more people having love and respect for Jesus Christ.

I share these reasons so you can better understand the issues.

So More People Will Read It

A book can be read anywhere, anytime. It can be read on a lunch break, on a vacation, or while traveling. A book can be read where there are no computers.

Many people in the world do not have Internet access yet. And not everyone who can access the Internet likes to read long articles or books on a computer. Many people prefer to read printed material they can hold in their hands.

So the way to insure the widest possible distribution is publishing a book — and putting the basic information on the Internet also. This is what we have done.

Books have their own separate ways of being promoted and distributed, such as book lists, book reviews, and libraries, that web articles lack.

Information is easier to share with others if it is in printed form. A web address is easy to share by email, but if you have to print off all the pages, it can be easier, and even cheaper, to buy a book — which is much nicer to have than a stapled bunch of papers printed from a web site.

Also, people can easily misplace, neglect, or forget a recommended web site, but a book sitting on their table will not be forgotten. Even if it gets covered up, it eventually will be seen again and thus remembered.

So People Will Value It

People have more respect for information written in a book than they do for an article on the Internet or even in a magazine. Books carry more weight in the minds of people.

A fact of human nature is that most people do not value what does not cost anything. They think, and rightly so most of the time, that if something is free it must not have much value. So offering something free can be a way to guarantee people will not value your information, and thus ignore it.

However, in this day we cannot ignore such a phenomenal method of spreading information as the Internet. So, the web site[1] is available so people can hear the basic arguments contained in the book, and easily share these ideas, so others can learn of the book.

---

1 www.LookingAtWomenIsNotASin.com

The main information in this book is given freely on the web without cost. Only those who wish to study the subject in more detail, or wish to have the information in book form will need to purchase the book. Anyone can learn the main points contained in the book without cost at the web site.

Book purchasers do receive additional valuable information, which will save them study time, because the additional chapters give more detail, making it easier to understand and believe the teaching of the book. Purchasers of the book also support the spread of these truths.

So It Can Be A Reference For The Future

A book can be kept, studied, read, and referred to repeatedly. You, or someone you know, will need to read this book again, sometime. This is probably the best argument for why you should buy this book.

The information in this book is something you need to have readily available for future reference. Not just so you can read it again, but as a resource to back up statements you will want to make to others based on these truths. Most people don't have perfect memories, especially after being exposed to material only once. A printed book, readily at hand, is a way to insure this vital information does not get away from you.

A book is much easier to keep and locate than any alternative. So a book makes the best format for owning and keeping information you will want, or need, to refer to again in the future.

Not Just To Make Money

There are costs involved with publishing a book, so they have to be covered somehow, and the obvious way is to have the readers pay for the book they receive.

It also takes money to live on while you study and do research on new books that need to be written to help people. And it even costs money to provide a "free" web site. That money has to come from somewhere.

I am not selling this book with the motive to make money, although I do not believe making money is wrong. I am doing it to help people know the truth, so they can be freed from bondage, and so they will love Jesus instead of turning away from Him because of believing a lie.

It would be wrong for me to publish a book based just on the idea of making money, without regard for whether the book might harm people. If I did that, I would be letting money be my god, determining what I should do. I certainly do not want that.

My objective is simply to see this information spread as far and as quickly as possible. The fact that we will profit is just an added blessing, one which we thank God for, and which will allow us to continue to make God's message available to people as widely and freely as possible.

I Pray It Is Not A Stumbling-Block

For a long while before deciding to publish this book, I struggled with the question of whether this information might have the potential to be a stumbling-block to some people, instead of a blessing. After much prayer I have peace and assurance that making this information as widely known as possible is the right thing to do, and what will be pleasing to my wonderful Lord, Jesus Christ.

I refuse to fear that this book will give people a license to sin. If we preach grace, some people may misunderstand and abuse it. But that does not mean we should quit preaching the truth of the Bible about God's grace.

Whatever God put in the Bible is what God desires people to clearly understand. Correcting a misunderstanding, so people can see the truth of what Jesus really said and meant, cannot be wrong.

For God's Benefit

A great number of Christian men are sinning against God by their rebellion. They believe it is wrong to look at women, yet they still do it. It is not a sin to look at women, but because these men believe it is a sin, they are in rebellion against what they think is God's will, when they look at women. So for them, looking at women is a sin, because they are rebelling against what they think is God's will — even though they are wrong.

> ROMANS 14:23 NLT
> 23 But if you have doubts about whether or not you should eat something, you are sinning if you go ahead and do it. For you are not following your convictions. If you do anything you believe is not right, you are sinning.

God made women so attractive to men that it is almost impossible for men not to look at women. So most Christian men are looking. They try not to look, but usually find it an impossible struggle. This book is an effort to inform Christian men of the truth — that looking at women is not a sin — so they will not be separated from fellowship with the Lord by unnecessary rebellion against God.

By telling men the truth in this book, it will stop this kind of sin. Sin separates man from God, which is not God's desire. Jesus gave His life to pay for all sin, so God would no longer have to be separated from mankind whom He loves.

For this reason this book is also for God's benefit.

So I place these truths in your hands, hoping you will also desire to share them with others, so they can know the truth and be set free. I pray the will of the Lord Jesus Christ be done.

Afterword

Dear Reader,

If you were blessed by this book, please make a list now of at least three men you know that you should share this book with.

Sons, brothers, fathers, friends, ministers — they all need to know the liberating truths in this book.

You can tell them about the web site,[1] where they can read the Introduction and Conclusion and order the book themselves. Or, send them a gift copy of this book.

Because of ignorance, millions of men are needlessly suffering condemnation and lack of fellowship with God because they feel they can never be good enough to please God. They believe they are spiritual failures, because they struggle with sexual thoughts and desires. They have been told their sex drive is evil and God frowns on them because of it.

So the devil has been able to get them to despair of ever being a "good Christian" and have God's blessing in their life. In this way the devil has robbed their faith.

---

1 www.LookingAtWomenIsNotASin.com

Many have even turned their back on God, thinking they would never be able to overcome having sexual temptations they were told were sins.

The sad truth is, it has all been a lie based on misunderstanding Scripture.

These men should be set free to enjoy the blessing of knowing Jesus Christ in truth, without the false guilt and shame that has hindered their spiritual lives.

Jesus loves these men and gave His life so they could be free and enjoy right standing with God because of faith in Him.

Not only have these men been robbed, but the church has been robbed of their strength. Most importantly, God has been robbed of many spiritual warriors through the devil's lie, which has been accepted because of a misunderstanding of Scripture.

Please share this message with those men you care about.

Thank you!

May God bless you!

Bibliography

[1] Countryman, L. William. Dirt Greed & Sex, Sexual Ethics in the New Testament and Their Implications For Today. Philadelphia: Fortress Press, 1988.

[2] Hendriksen, William. New Testament Commentary: Thessalonians, Timothy and Titus. Grand Rapids: Baker Book House, 1979.

[3] Jordan, Clarence. The Cotton Patch Version of Paul's Epistles. Chicago: Follett Publishing Company, 1968.

Index

A

adultery
  meaning 23-30
  not 25
  property rights 28

B

betrothed 24, 25, 26, 27
Bible
  languages 20
  translations 17, 19, 20, 22, 79
bologna 20
bride price 25, 27
bull-shooting 20

C

canines 19
Chihuahua 19
coke 19
concubine 27
Cotton Patch version 19
Countryman, L. William 29, 54
covet
  same as lust 39
coveting, not mental 45

D

desire
  not wrong 40

devils, doctrine of 46
disease 68
divorced woman 27
dogs, hot 19
dowry 25, 27

E

epithumeo 41, 45, 51, 52, 53
epithumia 52, 53

F

feelings, of God 64
forgiveness 56, 76, 77, 85

G

gluttony 47
guilty 9, 14, 74, 81, 82, 83, 87
gune 32
gyne 32, 33, 80

H

hamartia 55
Hendriksen, William 48
hush puppies 19

I

impatience 48
intent 14, 40

intention 38, 54

J

Jordan, Clarence 19
judgment, words 74

L

law
  ceremonial 71
  of God 83
  of love 46, 66, 68, 69
  Old Testament 13, 58, 68
lawlessness 58
lust
  meaning 35
  positive 41, 42
lusts, youthful 48

M

motives 14

P

paraphrase 19
Paul, apostle 22
polygamy 25
pornography 73
pregnant 68
pride 48, 69
prostitute 27

R

rebellion 48

S

selfishness 48, 66, 69, 70, 71
  turn Heaven to Hell 70
Septuagint 39, 51, 52, 81

sin
  against God 62
  comes from heart 73
  definition 55
  forgiveness of 56, 76, 77, 85, 86
  harmful 46, 56, 61, 65, 74
  missing the mark 55, 82
  not doing good 65
  not mental 72
  not of faith 64
single woman 25, 67
slave woman 27, 28, 29
sullambano 36

T

temptation
  not sin 36
  of Jesus 37
thoughts, not sin 46, 47, 60, 72, 74, 82
Torah 29
tradition 11, 12, 57, 82
translating 19
translations 17, 19, 20, 22, 79, 80
translators 17, 19, 31, 32, 49, 52
Tyndale, William 32

W

web site 89, 92, 93, 94, 97, 103
widow 27
wife 29, 32
  bethrothed already a 26
wives 32
woman 32
women 32

Y

youthful lusts 48

Ordering Information

This book may be purchased through Amazon.com. Additional information on ordering may be available at our web site:

www.LookingAtWomenIsNotASin.com

If you were helped or enlightened by reading this book, please consider leaving your comments at Amazon.com so others will be encouraged to read it.

www.ingramcontent.com/pod-product-compliance
Lightning Source LLC
Chambersburg PA
CBHW031258290426
44109CB00012B/642